DAILY WALKING

LOG BOOK

THIS BELONGS TO	
PHONE	EMAIL
LOGBOOK START DATE	LOGBOOK COMPLETE DATE

DATE	TIME	LOCATION	DISTANCE	STEPS	COMMENT

GOALS & NOTES

DATE	TIME	LOCATION	DISTANCE	STEPS	COMMENT

GOALS & NOTES

DATE	TIME	LOCATION	DISTANCE	STEPS	COMMENT

GOALS & NOTES

DATE	TIME	LOCATION	DISTANCE	STEPS	COMMENT

GOALS & NOTES

DATE	TIME	LOCATION	DISTANCE	STEPS	COMMENT

GOALS & NOTES

DATE	TIME	LOCATION	DISTANCE	STEPS	COMMENT

GOALS & NOTES

DATE	TIME	LOCATION	DISTANCE	STEPS	COMMENT

GOALS & NOTES

DATE	TIME	LOCATION	DISTANCE	STEPS	COMMENT

GOALS & NOTES

DATE	TIME	LOCATION	DISTANCE	STEPS	COMMENT

GOALS & NOTES

DATE	TIME	LOCATION	DISTANCE	STEPS	COMMENT

GOALS & NOTES

DATE	TIME	LOCATION	DISTANCE	STEPS	COMMENT

GOALS & NOTES

DATE	TIME	LOCATION	DISTANCE	STEPS	COMMENT

GOALS & NOTES

DATE	TIME	LOCATION	DISTANCE	STEPS	COMMENT

GOALS & NOTES

DATE	TIME	LOCATION	DISTANCE	STEPS	COMMENT

GOALS & NOTES

DATE	TIME	LOCATION	DISTANCE	STEPS	COMMENT

GOALS & NOTES

DATE	TIME	LOCATION	DISTANCE	STEPS	COMMENT

GOALS & NOTES

DATE	TIME	LOCATION	DISTANCE	STEPS	COMMENT

GOALS & NOTES

DATE	TIME	LOCATION	DISTANCE	STEPS	COMMENT

GOALS & NOTES

DATE	TIME	LOCATION	DISTANCE	STEPS	COMMENT

GOALS & NOTES

DATE	TIME	LOCATION	DISTANCE	STEPS	COMMENT

GOALS & NOTES

DATE	TIME	LOCATION	DISTANCE	STEPS	COMMENT

GOALS & NOTES

DATE	TIME	LOCATION	DISTANCE	STEPS	COMMENT

GOALS & NOTES

DATE	TIME	LOCATION	DISTANCE	STEPS	COMMENT

GOALS & NOTES

DATE	TIME	LOCATION	DISTANCE	STEPS	COMMENT

GOALS & NOTES

DATE	TIME	LOCATION	DISTANCE	STEPS	COMMENT

GOALS & NOTES

DATE	TIME	LOCATION	DISTANCE	STEPS	COMMENT

GOALS & NOTES

DATE	TIME	LOCATION	DISTANCE	STEPS	COMMENT

GOALS & NOTES

DATE	TIME	LOCATION	DISTANCE	STEPS	COMMENT

GOALS & NOTES

DATE	TIME	LOCATION	DISTANCE	STEPS	COMMENT

GOALS & NOTES

DATE	TIME	LOCATION	DISTANCE	STEPS	COMMENT

GOALS & NOTES

DATE	TIME	LOCATION	DISTANCE	STEPS	COMMENT

GOALS & NOTES

DATE	TIME	LOCATION	DISTANCE	STEPS	COMMENT

GOALS & NOTES

DATE	TIME	LOCATION	DISTANCE	STEPS	COMMENT

GOALS & NOTES

DATE	TIME	LOCATION	DISTANCE	STEPS	COMMENT

GOALS & NOTES

DATE	TIME	LOCATION	DISTANCE	STEPS	COMMENT

GOALS & NOTES

DATE	TIME	LOCATION	DISTANCE	STEPS	COMMENT

GOALS & NOTES

DATE	TIME	LOCATION	DISTANCE	STEPS	COMMENT

GOALS & NOTES

DATE	TIME	LOCATION	DISTANCE	STEPS	COMMENT

GOALS & NOTES

DATE	TIME	LOCATION	DISTANCE	STEPS	COMMENT

GOALS & NOTES

DATE	TIME	LOCATION	DISTANCE	STEPS	COMMENT

GOALS & NOTES

DATE	TIME	LOCATION	DISTANCE	STEPS	COMMENT

GOALS & NOTES

DATE	TIME	LOCATION	DISTANCE	STEPS	COMMENT

GOALS & NOTES

DATE	TIME	LOCATION	DISTANCE	STEPS	COMMENT

GOALS & NOTES

DATE	TIME	LOCATION	DISTANCE	STEPS	COMMENT

GOALS & NOTES

DATE	TIME	LOCATION	DISTANCE	STEPS	COMMENT

GOALS & NOTES

DATE	TIME	LOCATION	DISTANCE	STEPS	COMMENT

GOALS & NOTES

DATE	TIME	LOCATION	DISTANCE	STEPS	COMMENT

GOALS & NOTES

DATE	TIME	LOCATION	DISTANCE	STEPS	COMMENT

GOALS & NOTES

DATE	TIME	LOCATION	DISTANCE	STEPS	COMMENT

GOALS & NOTES

DATE	TIME	LOCATION	DISTANCE	STEPS	COMMENT

GOALS & NOTES

DATE	TIME	LOCATION	DISTANCE	STEPS	COMMENT

GOALS & NOTES

DATE	TIME	LOCATION	DISTANCE	STEPS	COMMENT

GOALS & NOTES

DATE	TIME	LOCATION	DISTANCE	STEPS	COMMENT

GOALS & NOTES

DATE	TIME	LOCATION	DISTANCE	STEPS	COMMENT

GOALS & NOTES

DATE	TIME	LOCATION	DISTANCE	STEPS	COMMENT

GOALS & NOTES

DATE	TIME	LOCATION	DISTANCE	STEPS	COMMENT

GOALS & NOTES

DATE	TIME	LOCATION	DISTANCE	STEPS	COMMENT

GOALS & NOTES

DATE	TIME	LOCATION	DISTANCE	STEPS	COMMENT

GOALS & NOTES

DATE	TIME	LOCATION	DISTANCE	STEPS	COMMENT

GOALS & NOTES

DATE	TIME	LOCATION	DISTANCE	STEPS	COMMENT

GOALS & NOTES

DATE	TIME	LOCATION	DISTANCE	STEPS	COMMENT

GOALS & NOTES

DATE	TIME	LOCATION	DISTANCE	STEPS	COMMENT

GOALS & NOTES

DATE	TIME	LOCATION	DISTANCE	STEPS	COMMENT

GOALS & NOTES

DATE	TIME	LOCATION	DISTANCE	STEPS	COMMENT

GOALS & NOTES

DATE	TIME	LOCATION	DISTANCE	STEPS	COMMENT

GOALS & NOTES

DATE	TIME	LOCATION	DISTANCE	STEPS	COMMENT

GOALS & NOTES

DATE	TIME	LOCATION	DISTANCE	STEPS	COMMENT

GOALS & NOTES

DATE	TIME	LOCATION	DISTANCE	STEPS	COMMENT

GOALS & NOTES

DATE	TIME	LOCATION	DISTANCE	STEPS	COMMENT

GOALS & NOTES

DATE	TIME	LOCATION	DISTANCE	STEPS	COMMENT

GOALS & NOTES

DATE	TIME	LOCATION	DISTANCE	STEPS	COMMENT

GOALS & NOTES

DATE	TIME	LOCATION	DISTANCE	STEPS	COMMENT

GOALS & NOTES

DATE	TIME	LOCATION	DISTANCE	STEPS	COMMENT

GOALS & NOTES

DATE	TIME	LOCATION	DISTANCE	STEPS	COMMENT

GOALS & NOTES

DATE	TIME	LOCATION	DISTANCE	STEPS	COMMENT

GOALS & NOTES

DATE	TIME	LOCATION	DISTANCE	STEPS	COMMENT

GOALS & NOTES

DATE	TIME	LOCATION	DISTANCE	STEPS	COMMENT

GOALS & NOTES

DATE	TIME	LOCATION	DISTANCE	STEPS	COMMENT

GOALS & NOTES

DATE	TIME	LOCATION	DISTANCE	STEPS	COMMENT

GOALS & NOTES

DATE	TIME	LOCATION	DISTANCE	STEPS	COMMENT

GOALS & NOTES

DATE	TIME	LOCATION	DISTANCE	STEPS	COMMENT

GOALS & NOTES

DATE	TIME	LOCATION	DISTANCE	STEPS	COMMENT

GOALS & NOTES

DATE	TIME	LOCATION	DISTANCE	STEPS	COMMENT

GOALS & NOTES

DATE	TIME	LOCATION	DISTANCE	STEPS	COMMENT

GOALS & NOTES

DATE	TIME	LOCATION	DISTANCE	STEPS	COMMENT

GOALS & NOTES

DATE	TIME	LOCATION	DISTANCE	STEPS	COMMENT

GOALS & NOTES

DATE	TIME	LOCATION	DISTANCE	STEPS	COMMENT

GOALS & NOTES

DATE	TIME	LOCATION	DISTANCE	STEPS	COMMENT

GOALS & NOTES

DATE	TIME	LOCATION	DISTANCE	STEPS	COMMENT

GOALS & NOTES

DATE	TIME	LOCATION	DISTANCE	STEPS	COMMENT

GOALS & NOTES

DATE	TIME	LOCATION	DISTANCE	STEPS	COMMENT

GOALS & NOTES

DATE	TIME	LOCATION	DISTANCE	STEPS	COMMENT

GOALS & NOTES

DATE	TIME	LOCATION	DISTANCE	STEPS	COMMENT

GOALS & NOTES

DATE	TIME	LOCATION	DISTANCE	STEPS	COMMENT

GOALS & NOTES

DATE	TIME	LOCATION	DISTANCE	STEPS	COMMENT

GOALS & NOTES

DATE	TIME	LOCATION	DISTANCE	STEPS	COMMENT

GOALS & NOTES

DATE	TIME	LOCATION	DISTANCE	STEPS	COMMENT

GOALS & NOTES

DATE	TIME	LOCATION	DISTANCE	STEPS	COMMENT

GOALS & NOTES

DATE	TIME	LOCATION	DISTANCE	STEPS	COMMENT

GOALS & NOTES

DATE	TIME	LOCATION	DISTANCE	STEPS	COMMENT

GOALS & NOTES

NOTES

NOTES

NOTES

NOTES

THANKYOU FOR YOUR PURCHASE!

If you get the chance, please consider leaving an honest review on Amazon. We appreciate every one

Made in the USA
Las Vegas, NV
13 August 2021